Ghetto Love
My
Version
Of
SEX
PAIN
&
LOVE

By
Sedelia Gardner

Avid Readers Publishing Group

Lakewood, California

The opinions expressed in this manuscript are those of the author and do not represent the thoughts or opinions of the publisher. The author warrants and represents that she has the legal right to publish or owns all material in this book. If you find a discrepancy, contact the publisher at www.avidreaderspg.com.

Ghetto Love

My Version of Sex, Pain & Love

All Rights Reserved

Copyright © 2011 Sedelia Gardner

This book may not be transmitted, reproduced, or stored in part or in whole by any means without the express written consent of the publisher except for brief quotations in articles and reviews.

Avid Readers Publishing Group

http://www.avidreaderspg.com

ISBN-13: 978-1-61286-042-8

Printed in the United States

Stop asking God to
Guide you if you
Are too lazy to
Open your
Eyes and
See the
PATH

Sedelia Gardner

Part 1
SEX

When it comes to expression there aren't really any rules to follow but one and that is to find your own flow so that you can be heard.

Sedelia Gardner

Tomatoes

Round nice and juicy
Plump and filled with juice
Hanging off a vine in the sunlight
Waiting for someone to pick
I will never forget my first bite

Sedelia Gardner

Tend to your Garden

Come tend to your garden
The valley is over grown with grass
And the river is hard to see

Come tend to your garden
Pull out your long grass shears
And cut the grass down low if you like

Come tend to your garden
The berries are ripe for the picking
Sweet juicy ready for your lips
But only if you're hungry

Come tend to your garden
Use your hoe and shovel
And toil over the packed soil to loosen it up
To help the water flow to the roots

Come tend to your garden
Pull out your packet of seeds
And sprinkle them upon the brown wet soil
If you like

Come tend to your garden
The soil is dry from neglect
The best time to water her is at night
Please water your garden as much as you like

Sedelia Gardner

Relax

Long black silky hair down past my shoulders spread out across
My back like eagle wings in the sky. Enjoying the touch of your
Hands but still I need to relax.

Hands run down to caress my breast with nipples hard as
Flower buds waiting to blossom open to the sunlight. I enjoy it
But still I need to relax.

Enjoying the look in your eyes as you admire the coco brown
Canvas in front of you. Carefully examining every piece but still
I need to relax.

Fingers run down to find a bush that covers my valley deep.
Hair moistening and glistening in the candle light looking like
Drops of dew on the morning grass. My head goes back as you
Dip down to take a sip but still I need to relax.

Thick thighs spread open to reveal a gate with a pink lock. You began
To pull out your key and I can feel you turning your key inside to see if
It fits. Enter the door is open wide stay for a while I need to relax!

Sedelia Gardner

Sounds of love

Come here enter me and glaze into my eyes as we began to orchestrate the
Sounds of love
Whisper in my ear and softly tell me what I need to hear to moan to you
The sounds of love
Touch me in the places where I need to be touched to sing out loud to you
The sounds of love
Hold me tight with a grip around my waist and listen to me echo the
Sounds of love
Kiss me with a heat of passion to help me release the sweet
Sounds of love
Join in and hold me tight let it go as we scream out the sounds of love

Sedelia Gardner

Georgia Peach

I watched you at the busy market place today
Slowly passing the other vendors by as you looked for that special one
Your eyes began to fill with delight as you spot it near
Nice and round a little bruised with a touch of soft fuzz
You quickly wipe it off and smile as you take your first bite
I watch you enjoy the taste of the hidden sweet juice
I smile back at you while you enjoy eating your Georgia Peach

Sedelia Gardner

A storm is coming

Emotions hit me like a lighting strike and thunder rumbles
Through my body it feels like a storm is coming

Heat fills my body and the heat waves travel through me like hot
Winds in the desert it feels like a storm is coming

Sweat beads quickly roll down my body flowing down reminding me
Of waves crashing in the open seas it feels like a storm is coming

My body tense up and shake like an after shock of an earthquake
I am not afraid I won't run it feels like a storm is coming

I can feel my insides rumble and boil over ready to flow like lava
From a volcano it's building up fast it feels like a storm is coming

My body twist and twine as if it were fighting against the winds
Of a tornado you grab my hand it feels like a storm is coming

There you are waiting for me standing strong against the storm
Aiming for the eye of the hurricane I am not moving I want to
Feel this storm coming

Sedelia Gardner

Fill my glass

It feels smooth as I lightly lick my fingers and
Began to run them around the circled rim
Tall, strong, slim but wide enough to
Hold what I need to be full
You smile as I enjoy the
Few drops on my lips
I began to glisten
As you again
Fill my
Glass
With
Wine

Sedelia Gardner

Take my Clothes off

Two brown mountains standing tall reminding you of Egyptians pyramids
Your tongue explore to reach the peaks as your hands slide between the
River cleavage that separates them

What are you waiting for take my clothes off

You slowly turn me over to explore the south the small of my back
Reminds you of a deep valley in the Grand Canyon as your fingers slowly
Glide to cross over the two hills

What are you waiting for take my clothes off

Legs long but your hands don't mind the travel the shade of brown skin
Reminds you of the desert sand of the Sahara luckily you find an oasis
And stop to take a sip

What are you waiting for take my clothes off

Heat fills the room as if there were sun rays escaping from my body
Sweat drips from your head like the rain in the Amazon

You'r moving to slow for me tonight I'll take my clothes off

Sedelia Gardner

Black Oil

You may look like a mine of
Silver
And to some look like a bar of
Gold
You may look like a bunch of
Diamonds
But your love flows in me like
Black oil

Sedelia Gardner

I wanna

You lay me back and let your tongue tease my dark brown nipples upon my breast
They stand out like ungrounded coffee beans oh how I enjoy every moment but
Don't keep me waiting I wanna make love tonight

I can feel you gently nibbling on my ear and your warm breath resting upon my
Neck and the feeling excites me as if it's our first time I am enjoying every minute of it
But don't keep me waiting I wanna make love tonight

Your tongue glides down across my body touching every inch of me to you it's
Perfect no words for how you admire me I enjoy every moment of it but don't
Keep me waiting I wanna make love tonight

You grab my thighs gently caressing them softly my calf muscles tighten up as you
Begin to suck on my toes oh I can feel my desire inside for you grow I am enjoying
Every minute of it but don't keep me waiting I wanna make love tonight

Your tongue slowly glides up my inner legs to drink
from a pool of ecstasy I can tell
Your thirsty as you sip from my water falls my dam
is about to burst I am enjoying
All of it but don't keep me waiting I wanna make
love tonight

Here you come dark brown like sweet chocolate
with a skin as smooth as silk flawless
I love this picture every time I see it I am enjoying
every second of it but don't keep me
Waiting I wanna make love tonight

Sedelia Gardner

Touch it

Touch it
And lay back and think of me
Relax breathe slow and be free
Touch it
Close your eyes and moan
You hear my voice in your ear so you're not alone
Touch it
And let me know how does it feel
Your getting hot so you know the feeling is real
Touch it
Is it soft like cotton and slippery like ice inside
Go slow and let your fingers slowly slide
Touch it
Your almost there don't stop relax
And let me hear you scream my name
Don't stop touch it
It felt good inside but it's still not the same

Sedelia Gardner

Two shades of brown

Two shades of brown wrapped together to form a perfect masterpiece
Arms wrapped around her body as he lay protecting his precious piece
Legs twined and twisted together like branches on a tree
Hands running across each other body enjoying the chance to be free
Touching places that are usually covered but today it's all bare
The sweet sounds of love making is echoing through this private lair
He's on top of her she's on top of him ecstasy is perfectly orchestrated together as one song spun
Beads of sweat dripping down resting on their bodies glistening in the morning sun
Leaves fall seasons change and a new life has just begun
Two shades of brown finally together as they become one

Sedelia Gardner

Magic ride

I'll like to take you on a trip around the world we can enjoy the smell of the
Ocean and watch the white foam form on the waves on the beach during
Sunset on our magic ride

Well maybe we can go to the Africa and take a journey through the many
Jungles and play in the Nile river and listen to the lions roar on this magic
Ride

If that is too much for you we can slow it down and hold hands in New York
City while taking a stroll through Central Park while on this magic ride

Or we can stretch our legs and take a mountain climb up Mount Fiji don't
Worry you won't fall I got your and on this magic ride

So close your eyes come and pull back the sheets and let your body glide
Across the silk sheets as if you were floating on a cloud as I take you on
Your magic ride

Sedelia Gardner

Money on the table

I can see you looking at me wondering who will make the
First move but it won't be me until you put the money on the
Table

You stand and walk around the room and examine the fine
Item in front of you but you won't make the first move
Until you put the money on the table

You slowly unbutton your shirt exposing to me a world of
Fantasy dam I won't make the first move until my money is
On the table

Your hand slowly reach into your pocket to pull out my
Motivation my robe drops to the floor as you put my
Money on the table

Sedelia Gardner

Knock the cob webs out

My body is feeling dirty as the cracks and crevices are filling up with dust
I need someone to come knock the cob webs out

My muscles in my legs are starting to ache they haven't been stretched in
A while I need someone to come knock the cob webs out

My breast are feeling tender to the touch a massage is long over due I
Need someone to come knock the cob webs out

My back is feeling stiff I have a few bones that need to be cracked I need
Someone to come knock the cob webs out

My hair is starting to tangle I haven't had any fingers run through it in a
While I need someone to come knock the cob webs out

My fingers are stiffing up feel like arthritis is setting in they haven't
Scratched in a while I need someone to come knock the cob webs out

My baby is busy working today I haven't seen him
since last night let me
Call 555-555-5555 to remind him to come knock
the cob webs out

Sedelia Gardner

Get you off

Standing here watching you take your morning shave inside I'm still
Enjoying last night pleasure it was good to me but I still have to get you off

Warm water beads cover your body as you take your shower steam fills
The air taking me back to the heat of last night it was good to me but I
Still have to get you off

My hands rub across your body drying up the water beads as I slowly kiss
The scratches on your back received from last night pleasure it was good
To me but I still have to get you off

Enjoying the look in your eyes as I slowly kiss everything that is mine I drop
To my knees as your fingers get tangled in my hair as I proceed to get you
Off

Sedelia Gardner

Pecan

There you are with a
Nice shade of brown
Laying upon the ground
Smooth to the touch
With a small crack
Waiting to be open like an untouched pecan

Sedelia Gardner

Pink lips

I gently toss the warm water around my lips
As I get them prepared for the day
Carefully removing any unwanted hair that
Surrounds them
They can only be one shade each and everyday
Then I enjoy his smile as he softly kiss my pink lips

Sedelia Gardner

WHAT

What would she do if she knew what I did to you

What would she do if she found out your love wasn't true

What would she do if she knew when she kissed your lips she was kissing mine to

What would she do if she knew you pleased me to

And that your lips kissed my place a time or to

And that we went to that special place just me and you

But what would you do if you knew I was pleasing her to

Sedelia Gardner

Waist down

Touch me there
Go slow because that's the way I like it
Hold me close
For a moment as if you really need me
All that matters right now is that
You know my name
From the waist down

Whisper in my ear
And let's pretend that I'm your one and only
Come closer and
Run your hands all over my body like you miss me
Don't hesitate all that matters right now is that
You know my name
From the waist down

Kiss my lips
As if we have done this a hundred times before
Close your eyes
And let's pretend that I'm the one you're thinking of
I don't mind all you need to know is my name
From the waist down

Let the music play
And we can pretend like this is our song
Let my name roll off of your lips
Like it's a routine
It's not hard to say when it gets good
You know my name
From the waist down

Sedelia Gardner

You can see back
Into my past
And be with me
Among my present
But you can not
Determine my future

Sedelia Gardner

Part 2
PAIN

Everyone knows a monster but a monster can only stay a monster when he has some where to hide.

Laying in a pool of tears

Here I am laying in a pool of tears
   So deep I am almost drowning
      But there is no life guard in sight
         The water seem shallow
            But once you get in it's deeper than an ocean
               And there is no way to touch the bottom

Here I am laying in a pool of tears
   But my eyes are as clear as the blue sky
      But the tears are falling out of my eyes
         Like a water falls

Here I am can you see me laying in a pool of tears
   As you touch my body to satisfy your inner most desire
         You kiss my lips as if it were the last time
            You scream my name to reassure me that you are all mine
               But when it is all over and the excitement is all gone
                  I am still left here laying in a pool of tears

Sedelia Gardner

Deceit

How did you mingle in and hide an evil in your eye
that only my eyes
Could see
You hid it very well to mingle with this family
How could you hold it in and slip away with an evil
in your eye that
Only my eyes could see
You must have practice very well to blend in with
this family
How could you pretend to love me in front of this
family while hiding
An evil in your eye that only my eyes could see
You played every part very well to stay a part of this
family
But one day your curtain will fall with an evil
everyone can see

Sedelia Gardner

Empty Room

It's a beautiful home from the inside and out nicely
painted and freshly cut yard laced
With rose bushes and inside the house is laid with
flat screens and leather couches and
Cherry wood tables were two people not speaking
sit in an empty room

Children run through the house yelling and
screaming at the top of their lungs even the dog
Join in and jump up on the furniture to take a nap
were the two people not speaking sit in
An empty room

The pizza has just been delivered and the kids are
fighting over who will get the first slice
Grape soda spills on the white carpet were the two
people not speaking sit in an empty room

Its night time and the children are laid down for bed
the night air feels colder than usual and a
Draft sweeps through to were the two people not
speaking sit in an empty room

Sedelia Gardner

Fallen on deaf ears

Reality has just sat in and it is eating my flesh down to the bone
Here I am surrounded by millions to see but I am in this world alone
My screams are echoing through the air in despair hoping all is not gone

Do you hear me? Have my efforts fallen on deaf ears?

Pain sits in and plays upon my weak body and shatters every bone
All eyes on me but why are they blind and leave me in this world alone
My screams are getting louder for everyone to hear but I fear their souls
Are gone

Do you hear me? Have my efforts fallen on deaf ears?

No more strength left in me my body is drained to the bone
People stop and stare but they don't see that I am beaten, tired and
Alone my screams are getting weaker not another sound to make my hope is
Gone

All my efforts have been in vain for they have fallen on deaf ears

Sedelia Gardner

One day

One day your gonna look for me
But you won't find me
One day your gonna need my voice
But you won't hear me
One day your gonna cry alone
But you won't find me
One day your gonna feel cold
But you won't feel my touch
One day your gonna scream out loud
But you won't see me
One day your gonna be alone
But you won't find me

Sedelia Gardner

There's a monster in my bed

There's a monster in my bed as I go running to my mother arms showing her
Fear that only a mother eye can see but she I blinded and she cannot see
There's a monster in my bed

There's a monster in my bed as I grab my father's arm to me he is the
Strongest man in the world but he is tired from work and his eyes are blurry
And he cannot see there's a monster in my bed

There's a monster in my bed as I hug my grandmother but she is too busy complaining
About how she doesn't like my mother and I am a child her eyes cannot see and she
Doesn't care if there is a monster in my bed

There's a monster in my bed and I'll face it alone and close my eyes and drift off to a
Far away world untouched and a secret place that only my eyes can see while there's
A monster in my bed

Sedelia Gardner

Wounded

My tears flow from my eyes but your hands reach
out and catch them so I
Am not left
Wounded
I am surrounded by so many puddles but you
quickly kneel down and soak
Them up
Open wounds cover my body that no one had tried
to stitch but you stay so I
Am not left
Wounded
My back is nearly broken and I cannot stand and my
legs can barely walk
But you come and give me leverage like an invisible
cane so I
Am not left
Wounded

Sedelia Gardner

Grains of sand

Here I am watching
As my pain slowly
Passes through me
Like an hour glass
All the pain is
Finally about to
Empty out then
Someone comes along
And turn the hour glass
Upside down again to
Cause my pain to drop
Again through me like
Grains of sand in an hour glass

Sedelia Gardner

Fear

Alone in a quiet room surrounded
By a sea of darkness and covered
By a mist of fear

I sit screaming in an empty
Chamber that no one else can hear

Scars so deep that they have cut
Through my very soul leaving me
With nothing but pain and fear

Defeat fills my body as my
Screams fills the room that
Only he can hear

I am bound down by a demon that
Only my eyes can see he likes
That and he can smell my fear

I'm tired as I watch the blood
Seep through my wounds as my
Soul slips away and my screams
I no longer hear

Sedelia Gardner

Far away

I want to fly up high way about the night stars
Step on the moon or dance around the rings of Saturn
And lay back and enjoy the warm rays from the Sun
Maybe even find a way to escape out of the Milky Way
Go some were far away and find a place just for me
Maybe travel past Pluto
Maybe I will get my wish today as I make my heart stop

Sedelia Gardner

Invisible

Here I am standing in front of you but your eyes look through me
Like I am not there I must be
Invisible
Do you hear my voice whispering in your ear to tell you how much I
Love you I get no response I must be
Invisible
Do you feel me touch your body as you lay across the silk sheets on
The bed you don't move I must be
Invisible
Here I am withering away like a flower in harvest time you past me
By without a care I must be
Invisible
You leave no words spoken no kiss no hug no goodbye the door
Slams shut I must be
Invisible

Sedelia Gardner

No one

Your touch feels like lightening flashing through my body but the pain
Feels so sweet
Vibrations roll through my body like thunder rumbling across the sky
Filling my body with a desired heat

Our lips touch melting me down like a freshly lit candle
I have asked for it in so many ways making sure I would be able to
Handle

All that you have to offer me in this precious moment as we become one is
A whirlwind of emotions building up inside of me wanting to be released
From this web we have just spun

I can feel your fingers slide slowly through my hair
As you enjoy my lips touching your body everywhere

I lay back waiting to receive what you have to offer me as I receive it with a moan
Only to wake up and face reality I am still alone

Sedelia Gardner

Alone

Rain drops rolling down the window reminding me
of the blood that flows through my veins

Emotions for you got me wrapped up and bound
with an unbreakable invisible chain

Love boiling for you at my finger tips like lava
inside a volcano waiting to flow

But the void in your heart is laced with trenched and
a ground I can never sow

All that is ms and all that is mine I pour so freely
into you only to watch it drip through the cracks
like small drops of dew

Touching you, holding you, caressing you and still
were both lonely still searching for something more

Sunlight beaming through the cracks marks the
beginning of a new day for some but for me a new
door

Sedelia Gardner

If I …..

If I could kill your soul a million times I would
never be satisfied

If I could slice you open with wounds and let the
vultures pick your flesh to the bone
I maybe a little happy but I still wouldn't be
satisfied

If I could rattle your body with a million bullets and
watch you fall lifelessly to the floor
I may clap my hands but I still wouldn't be satisfied

If I could tie you down and cut your wrist and watch
the blood drip from your arms
I may smile but I wouldn't be satisfied

If I could pull your eyes from their sockets and
watch you walk blindly around the world
I may jump for joy but I still wouldn't be satisfied

If I could burn you at the stake and listen to you
scream for mercy I may laugh a little but
I wouldn't be satisfied

If I could turn back the hands of time and erase my
mind would you still kill my soul to be satisfied

Sedelia Gardner

Where did you come from

You must have escaped from the depths of hell there is no way my
 merciful God would let you out
To come upon me like a thief in the night to ravage me, deceive me,
and rip me up from the inside out
where did you come from hiding out like a prisoner on the run
there is no way in hell my precious God would let you out
to come upon me like a butcher ready for the morning slaughter
to gut me open from the inside out
you must have lied your way out of your eternal hell there is no
way my merciful God would let you out

Sedelia Gardner

ALL

All I wanted to be was
>> First sometimes
>> Loved and maybe even
>> Thought of

All I needed to be was
>> First sometimes
>> Loved and maybe even
>> Thought of

All I accepted was
>> Last place
>> Being lied to and even
>> Ignored

All I got was
>> Last place
>> Being lied to and even
>> Ignored

Falling

Can you hear me screaming can you hear me
screaming to you
I'm falling

Here I am blowing in the wind like a leaf from a
tree during Autumn
Body worn and brittle like the twigs on the ground
being crushed beneath my feet

Can you hear me screaming can you hear me
screaming to you
I'm falling

Here I am floating in the air like a snowflake in the
air during Winter
Blood frozen and my heart is cold and hard like the
ground beneath my feet

Can you hear me screaming can you hear me
screaming to you
I'm falling

Here I am reaching for the sun like a flower bud
waiting to bloom during Spring
My back bends and raise again like the green grass
beneath my feet

Can you hear me screaming can you hear me
screaming to you
I'm falling

Here I am trying to stand against the wind like a
seagull flying in the sky during Summer
I am all dried up and there is nothing else to give so
I will dry up and float away like the dirt
Beneath my feet

Can you hear me screaming can you hear me
screaming to you
I'm falling

Sedelia Gardner

Look at the picture you painted

You wanted me to be pretty to remind you of my father

So God blessed you with me an image of my father

You wanted me to have hair like my father

So I was blessed with a crown of locks like my father

You wanted me to hold in pain just like you

So when I cried I cried inside to please you

You wanted me to smile just like you

So when I was beaten I smiled just to please you

You wanted me to have a sense of humor like my father

So I tried to make you laugh just like my father

You wanted me to be smart just like my father

So I never asked for help just like my father

You wanted me to protect the family just like you

So I let them abuse me just like you

You wanted me to sit alone in a corner just like you

So I wouldn't know how to ask for help just like you

You wanted me to be strong just like my father

So whenever I fell I got back up just like my father

You got everything you wanted so hang up the picture you painted

Sedelia Gardner

Good Bye

I still think about you
Even through the tears my thoughts still drift to you
Sometimes when I remise
I could almost feel that touch that I miss

I still think about you
Even thou the wound is deep my heart still wants you
I could almost imagine your lips upon me
Even through the pain with you is where I want to be

I still think about you
Even thou you don't want me with you
Sometimes I call your name at night
I sit longing for something that isn't right

I still think about you
Even thou I can't have you
Sometimes I hold on to memories and cry
I could move on if I could say goodbye

Sedelia Gardner

Ashes

Sometimes I feel like …….

God is looking down on me ……

And his light is beaming down on me …..

And burning my flesh from my bones ….

And I feel no pain as I leave here …

But his gentle breeze come and blows by ..

Causing my ashes to float among his wonders.

Sedelia Gardner

Why don't you comfort me

Come dry my eyes when my tears fall
Rub my back in time of pain
Share your love with me when I need it most
Comfort me

Come whisper to me in the darkness
Let me know that I'm not alone
Hold me so I'll know your close
Comfort me

Come look in my eyes
Let me see if I can find myself
Deep down inside your soul
Comfort me

Come feel my body with the
Warmth you have inside
I'm cold
Why don't you comfort me

Sedelia Gardner

I know that I am gone from you
And the distance that separates us
Is very far but the phone calls and
Text messages reassure you that your
On my mind but remember my body is
Distant but my heart is near

Part 3
LOVE

Pictures are priceless because that is a rare moment and you want to capture it right then.
But words are one of the most powerful forces on earth once the ink leaves the pen!

Sedelia Gardner

Don't Cry For Me

Don't cry for me
Whenever you need to see my smile I want you to
look up at the bright skies
Don't cry for me
Whenever you need to feel my warm touch I want
you to stand in the sunlight
Don't cry for me
Whenever you need to feel me pushing you I want
you to close your eyes
And left the wind blow up against your body
Don't cry for me
Whenever you need to hear a strong word of
encouragement from me
I want you to open the bible and read a verse
Don't cry for me
Whenever you need to hear me sing I want you to
go outside and
Listen to the birds chirping in the trees
Don't cry for me
Whenever you need to see my eyes I want you to go
outside in the night and
Look up at the stars sparkling in the sky
Don't cry for me
My body has now withered back to dust and my
soul is now resting in my father's arms

Whatever you do
Don't cry for me

Sedelia Gardner
Rest in Peace
Allen Gardner Jr.
12-31-2005

Broken wings

The burdens place upon my back kept me tied down to the ground
Until finally one day they broke my angel wings

I tried so hard to take flight to fly above the skies but things just kept
Me down and I never even had the strength to heal my broken wings

The tears fell from my eyes and it kept my body weak no matter how
Much I drank I could never find the strength to fly with my broken wings

My head felt so heavy and the light I could not see and there was no one
Else around I felt so alone stuck down on the ground with my broken wings

Then one day you came and I don't even know how and dried my tears and
My eyes refused to cry again and you gave me strength to heal my broken wings

The light I can now see and you got me far off of the ground and there is nothing
Holding us back down on the ground as we spread out our angel wings

Sedelia Gardner

In my bed

Another cold and lonely night while I am here laying in my bed
I'm holding on to my pillow wishing it was you instead
Caressing me holding me loving me here in my bed
I'm wondering if I am on your mind or if there is someone else instead
Laying here playing back memories of us in my head
While I'm laying here in my bed
I'm wondering if you love me too or if there is someone else instead
Remembering how you use to hold me tight while laying here in my bed
Do you ever remise about me or something else instead
Your touches make me warm inside while we are together laying here in my bed
Do you still want me like I want you or is there someone else instead
I can still smell your scent upon my sheets while laying here in my bed
Another long and lonely night for both of us instead

Sedelia Gardner

Diamond in the rough

Pull out your tools and come slowly chisel me out
this unfound black
Diamond in the rough
Come and unbound me from this lonely life of
darkness I have had enough
Shine me up and see the valued worth of this
unfound black
Diamond in the rough
Show me all the love you have to give me I want it
all because I will never
Get enough
Lift me up and wear like a jewel piece this unfound
black
Diamond in the rough
Bluff out my scars and wax my wounds I have worn
them long enough
Hold on to me and don't let go I don't want to be
lost again this unfound black
Diamond in the rough

Sedelia Gardner

Remise

You touched me and I began to melt
I want to remember how your first touch felt

You kiss me and my soul screams but you can't hear the sounds
I touch you and I can feel the joy inside me the harder my heart pounds

We caress and I loosen your belt
I want to remember this moment and how your first touch felt

I feel your hands slowly going up my thighs
Then you stop and take a pause as we get lost in each other eyes

You touched me and I began to melt
I want to remember how your first touch felt

You kiss me like no one has done before
My legs are open I'm ready and I want more

I'm sitting here thinking about how you touched me and
I began to melt while remising about how your first touch felt

Sedelia Gardner

In my heart

You curse at me and I curse at you harsh words causing deadly pain
But in my heart I never want to say good bye

      I hate you and you hate me too

You grab your things and pack them all away never to come back again
But in my heart I never want to say good bye

      I slam a door and you slam one too

You tell me you don't love me anymore and your can't take being around me
I throw back your ring but in my heart I never want to say good bye

      I walk away and you walk away too

You jump into your car and pull off leaving me with tears in my eyes as
An empty space but in my heart I never want to say good bye

Sedelia Gardner

Still waters ……..

After the drops fall the rain will come and then the storm will you still be there for me

Stand right beside me and cover me in battle

The waters are still not a ripple on the surface and your content

A few pebbles fall in and cause just enough waves to shake you

But you do nothing but draw me in closer to you

I feel the wind blow by and gently ruffle my hair

A little ripple form in our still waters

But you just stand in front of me letting the winds blow against your body

While protecting me I stop and stare in eyes so deep I see no bottom

And wonder how much more you can bare to keep still waters

Sedelia Gardner

Falling

I'm hanging over the side of a cliff fingers tired so I
let go and let myself
Fall into this endless pit
I'm fighting to catch my breath as gravity pulls me
down

I'm falling fast and it's for a man I don't even know

My heart is beating fast and my chest feels like it is
about to explode
I'm moving fast there is nothing to hold me back so
I'm letting go

I'm falling fast and it's for a man I don't even know

To weak to turn around but strong enough to keep
going on but the pit
Is endless
But I can see his face in front of me and hear his
voice in my ear

I'm falling fast and it's for a man I don't even know

I can't stop the fall and my feelings are to strong to
even slow it up
The pit is endless and I never want to hit the bottom

I'm falling fast and it's a man I don't even know

Sedelia Gardner

Something different

I am a breath of fresh air rolling in off the waves of the ocean

Inhale deeply and let my scent circulate through your veins

I see you smile this must be something different

I am like the tree that stands tall against the storm

Grab hold of my branches and hang up some of your burdens

I see you blushing this must be something different

I am like the mountain that refuses to crumble over time

Stand behind me so I can protect you from the things that come your way

I see you smile this must be something different

I am like the waters that run down the river and washes old deposits away

Don't run relax and enjoy something different

Sedelia Gardner

Will you remember

Will you remember to be my man or will I have to hammer rusty nails around
Your trunk to shock you to remind you that our job is to grow

Will you remember to be my man or will I have to lock up all my secrets and
Hide my feelings around my heart to confuse you to remind you that we both need trust

Will you remember to be my man or will I have to let my eyes wonder to look around
To anger you to remind you that we both need love

Will you remember to be my man or will I have to get guns and dogs to guard our home
To remind you that your job is to protect

Before I take another step with you will you remember to be my man

Sedelia Gardner

Perfect Man

A man made perfect without trials is that what you seek

Smooth hands tell me that he doesn't know how to work

No tattoos tells me that he can't take a little pain in his life

Watching his speech when he talks tells me he is scared to be himself

No dirt on his shoes tells me he doesn't know how to get dirty

Background check all clear tells me when the time come he can't get his hussle on

No old battle wounds scars or old stitch marks tells me he has no backbone

A man made perfect without trials is impossible to seek

Sedelia Gardner

Water drops

The
Water is
Nice and cold
As I pass you the
Glass you lift the glass
Up and began to take a long
Gulp happy with the satisfaction
As some moisture is left on your lips
To sparkle like a small water drop

Sedelia Gardner

Long time

It's been a long time since I have gotten lost in your eyes now I see
Them again and it seems like the first time

I get lost for a while smelling the scent of your cologne I have missed
That so much it's been a long time

It's been a long time since your hands have danced across my body it
Reminds me of the first time

I kiss you like we have never met before this feeling seems new to me
It's been a long time

Sedelia Gardner

Today

Looking in a mirror trying to decide which woman should I be today

Picking up the towel wash the sleep from my eyes and begin to mold myself like untouched clay

Should I let my hair down relax and let society see me today

Or pin it up tight holding in the scars inside and search for a quiet place to pray

Should I relax my throat and let the words flow freely today

Or put on my 9 – 5 voice and think about what I need to say

Long ponytail, afro, kinky twist or braids, black, blonde or red which one today

Or should I play it safe because I know I have bills to pay

Almost done empty back pack strapped on ready to be filled with the struggles of today

Thank god I have faith so come what may

Sedelia Gardner

Trapped heat

Your breath expels from your mouth
   And drapes my body in a unseen cloth of happiness
      It feels like silk as it glides across my body
         Trapping my heat inside

Small tears drop from your brown eyes
  And splash down against my breast
     It feels like a rain storm as the drops hit my body
       Trapping my heat inside

Lovely words escape from your lips
  And tangle my mind in a giant spider web of delight
     It feels like steel rods wrapped around my body
       Trapping my heat inside

Sedelia Gardner

When you're gone

I'm laying here in bed listening to the quiet storm
and I hear
Our favorite song I began to remise and start to get
warm inside
But it doesn't mean anything when you're gone

I got my hair down today I'm wearing it down just
how you like it
New French manicure and my toes painted to but it
doesn't
Mean anything when you're gone

I have a new outfit white sweater and some tight
jeans with a new
Pair of high heeled boots I look fine as hell but it
doesn't
Mean anything when you're gone

It's night time now and I slip into some new lingerie
white lace with the string
In the back nicely placed I'm starting to feel warm
inside as I began to remise
But it doesn't mean nothing when you're gone

Sedelia Gardner

You

Ghetto tats spread out across your body to tell a story of your life that's what I
Like and that's what I remember about you
Bald head smooth to the touch as my fingers glide across it like I'm sliding on
Ice I like that and that's what I remember about you
Arms nicely cut and strong enough to hold me tight and I like that and that's
What I remember about you
Deep brown eyes so sincere with a child like innocence but strong enough to
Pull me in your life mesmerizing and that's what I remember about you
Broad chest perfectly arranged hairless smooth to the touch like finished
Marble that's what I like and that's what I remember about you
You smile and I see your gold grill to remind me of the thug you are and it's
Sexy as hell and that's what I like and that's what I remember about you
Legs long and slim but strong enough to get the job done right and I like that
And that's what I remember about you
Lips softer than the clouds in the sky I remember how they felt upon my body
And I like that and that's what I remember about you

Hands strong as steel but smooth like a cut diamond
I love the touch and that's
What I remember about you
A perfect shade of brown dark as morning coffee
without the cream I like that
And that's what I remember about you

Sedelia Gardner

How did you get here

I thought I had a gate up
Strong and unbreakable
With no key and no way
In and no way out one
Day I seen you walking
Quietly in the halls
Holding a torch for
Us too see as I
Wonder how did
You get here

Sedelia Gardner

I can be ….

Please don't look at my rags

I can be the perfect gem if you take time to rub me and polish me

I can be a priceless pink diamond if you take your time to find how rare I am

I can be as shiny as a fresh water pearl if you take the time to clean me off

I can be stronger that titanium steel if you take the time to open the door and let me in

I can be as solid as a bar of gold if you take your time to see who I am

Please don't look at my rags just take your time to dust them off

Sedelia Gardner

Thinking

Here I remember you standing in front of me naked and exposed only to my light

Your eyes are looking at me amazed and astonished while I admire this perfect sight

Kissing you felt like heaven on earth and I wanted to spread my wings and began to take flight

Here I remember you for the first time slowly touching me the feeling to me was so right

I am so sad glazing into the sun thinking about you tonight

Sedelia Gardner

Do you love me

Do you love me
Are the words I ask everyday
Do you love me
Are the easiest words to say but the hardest ones to prove
Do you love me
Are words that can build a foundation or crumble a foundation
Do you love me
Are words that can cover up scars etched deep inside
Do you love me
Are words that can fall upon your ears in the heat of passion
Do you love me
Are words that have been spoken since the beginning of time
Do you love me
Are words I hear but long to feel
Do you love me
Are words I search for every time I look into your eyes
Do you love me
Are words that can bind you into a lifetime of hell or an eternity in heaven
Do you love me
Are words that can open a door or shut it close
Do you love me

Sedelia Gardner

Heels and tie

My eyes open to the morning sun and I hear my
kids calling my name its
Time for me to get into action and slip into my heels

I take a glance at my bills that are due today I take a
last look in the mirror
And adjust my attitude and put on my suit and tie

On my way to work to put in for my 9 – 5 suit
looking tight skirt just above
The knee let me adjust my attitude and slip into my
heels

Work is over its time to cook dinner and listen to the
kids tell stories of their
Day and remind them to do their homework and
how important they are to me
Let me adjust my attitude and slip on my suit and
tie

It's night time I need to pray and take a few
moments out for myself I look in the
Mirror I see a few gray hairs, some new wrinkles
and bags starting to form under
My eyes but it's time to rest I kick off my heels and
hang up suit and tie

Sedelia Gardner

Cinderella Shoe

There they all go dark, light and tan
Walking busily and passing her bye
Each day with a shoe in hand

She goes and takes a look in the mirror
And wonders why they pass her bye
And don't even stop to measure her foot

Maybe it's not her day to get her Cinderella shoe

Sedelia Gardner

Cornrows

Three strains of hair bind together as one to make cornrows
Long hair, short hair, black or brown, coarse, thick or thin can
Be turned into cornrows
No other race but mine has been blessed to wear these unique
Cornrows
Before there were weaves, perms, hair dye or wigs our beauty
Was enhanced by cornrows
So I will walk down the street happily and let the others envy my
Cornrows

Sedelia Gardner

Rib

I was told that I was made from a rib of a man
I tried to find my place in other broken ribs
But I would just break off and I couldn't stay in place
I tried to bandage the rib up, tape it up and even glue it up
But the rib would just continue to split
Attached to you is where I want to be
And if our rib began to crack I will pray it won't split

Sedelia Gardner

Cleopatra eyes

There she is slowly gliding across the Egyptian sands
Skin smooth and glistening like the sand she walks upon
Men bowing down to her feet as she passes them bye
Her scent is breath taking something he has never smelled
Her hair is in a style his eyes have never seen before
And the long rows of black silky hair with beads on the end has
Caught his attention
He has all the treasures in Rome
But there is nothing that can be crafted by hand that can be more
Precious than Cleopatra eyes

Sedelia Gardner

Beyond Sex

Can you take me to a place beyond sex baby
To a place where my ears don't hear the moans but my body still shakes
Can you fly me to a place beyond sex
To a place where my body isn't warm from the sheets but I still can feel your presence covering me
Can you show me a place beyond sex
To a place where our eyes don't meet but I can still feel you watching me even when you're not there
Can you wrap your hands around my body baby and take me to a place beyond sex
To that place I never been before where you are far from me but you always feel close
Can you take me to that place beyond sex
Just to reassure me there is not one else but me and you

Sedelia Gardner

Love me slow

Lately it's been all about you and I just feel like I
am being neglected so if it's not too much to ask
I was wondering if you could love me slow tonight

Take me and peel each layer of me off like an onion
and even when your eyes began to cry I want you to
continue peeling the layers because it's just another
piece of me that you need to know so
Can you please love me slow tonight

If crying is to much for you then maybe you can
pick me apart like a molecular structure and slowly
break down each molecule and when it seem to
complicated I don't want you to give up each
molecule if a piece of me that you need to know so
can you love me slow tonight

But I know how laid back you are so maybe you
can take a drive in your car down a long stretch of
highway and each mile that you past is a piece of
me and even when your car runs out of gas I want
you to be man enough to walk the rest of the miles
because each mile is a piece of me that you need to
know so do you think you can love me slow tonight

Sedelia Gardner

Other woman

Here I am sitting at home looking out the window waiting on you
You are probably
                Holding her
                              Kissing her

Caressing her

Or even loving her

But you could be telling her the same things that you whisper in my ear when
We lay in bed
                I care about you so much
                                      I will never leave you

There is no one else but you

        Or I love you

But for now I will sit at home and wait until I no longer decide to be the other woman

Sedelia Gardner

Someone else's

There he is with a six pack
Looks like they were chiseled out of stone by the ancient masters
Those stomach muscles intertwining perfectly as they carry me away
To visions of the Great Wall of China
Bronze skin beaming as the sunlight bounces off of his sweat
Those arms are long nice and strong
Reminding me of the strong African jungle vines
Legs sculpted precisely and every muscle is where it is suppose to be
Standing tall but sticking out like the old roots of a giant Oak tree
Bronze skin beaming as the sunlight bounces off of his sweat
Those dark brown eyes can take me anywhere
Make me dive in the great deep blue ocean
Those teeth bring out a captivating smile
Looking like ice glaciers surrounded by land
I sit here in a daze while day dreaming about someone else's man

Sedelia Gardner

Secret Pleasure

From the first moment I laid in your arms,
I knew it was a feeling I didn't want to lose
Feeling of unconditional love rush through my body,
And filled me with a secret pleasure that
 I know I can't share

Our lips have met a thousand times,
But each time they meet it feels as if it's the first time
I have laid in your arms and went to my
Secret place and embraced my secret pleasure that
I know I can't share

Just the thought of what I feel for you,
Fill my eyes with tears and bind my chest with feelings
I cannot yet express in words but its fills me with
That secret pleasure that
I know I can't share

Your eyes I have looked in time and time again
But each time I look into your eyes I find myself
Lost and wondering in my secret place and wrapped up
In my secret pleasure that only you can give that
I know I can't share

Enjoying the soft touch of your hands as they run,
Across my skin and go through my hair making
Me feel as if it were the first time I have ever been
touched
By you and praying inside it's not last as I enjoy my
secret pleasure
I know I can't share

Sedelia Gardner

Ghetto Love

I see you posted up on the corner with your jeans
hanging low with a
New white wife beater on to let your tattoos show I
see you sporting your
Bling while giving your hood some ghetto love

I walk past you with a swagger real slow got my
low rider jeans on so my
g-string can show the sunlight is beaming off of my
gold hoop ear rings
while I throw you up some ghetto love

You walk up behind me and post me up against the
wall kissing all my
Exposed place you got a firm grip so I know I won't
fall I know it's not
Proper and it's sure as hell isn't right but I'm gonna
let me head hang
Back while you embrace me with some ghetto love

Sedelia Gardner

Even after I gave my all I never got what I wanted never even tasted what I needed but when I stand before God at the end of my life I would hope that I would not have a single bit of talent left and could say I used everything you gave me.

Sedelia Gardner

www.ingramcontent.com/pod-product-compliance
Lightning Source LLC
Chambersburg PA
CBHW031412040426
42444CB00005B/530